D1187368

PHANTASIE

Sybille Pearson

357 W 20th St., NY NY 10011
212 627-1055

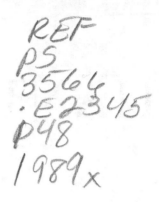

PHANTASIE

First printing: December 1989
ISBN: 0-88145-079-0

Book design: Marie Donovan
Word processing: WordMarc Composer Plus
Typographic controls: Xerox Ventura Publisher,
Professional Extension
Typeface: Palatino
Printed on acid-free paper and bound in the USA.

PHANTASIE was presented as part of (Baltimore) Center Stage's Playwrights '86 Series.

PHANTASIE received its world premiere on 3 January 1989 at the Vineyard Theater, New York City.
Doug Aibel was the Artistic Director, Barbara Zinn Krieger the Executive Director, and Jon Nakagawa the Managing Director. The cast and creative contributors were as follows:

D .... Diane Salinger
LEAH .... Elzbieta Czyzewska
VALERIE .... Laurinda Barrett
MICHAEL .... Michael French
LORRAINE .... Myra Taylor
DOCTOR .... Ryan Cutrona

Director .... John Rubinstein
Scenic design .... William Barclay
Lighting design .... Phil Monat
Costume design .... Deborah Shaw
Sound design .... Phil Lee
Production stage manager .... Shannon Graves

CHARACTERS

D, *a 35-year-old woman*
LEAH, *a 65-year-old woman, D's adoptive mother*
VALERIE, *a 53-year-old woman, D's natural mother*
MICHAEL, *a 35-year-old man, D's husband*
LORRAINE, *a 30–35-year-old black woman, and all other women characters*
DOCTOR, *a 40–50-year-old man, and all other men characters*

SETTING

The set is an open stage consisting of different settings: A corner of D's home, a corner of LEAH's home, a hotel lobby, and a cleared center stage to be used for other locations. The areas are defined by light. Each one is defined by a distinguishing light: A desk lamp for D's home, a standing lamp for LEAH's home, an electric sign that says THE BENTICK HOTEL for the lobby.

Lights also define D's fantasies; either a follow spot or specials can be used.

The play travels over the year and a half of D's search.

It starts on the day of the reunion.

ACT ONE

PLACE: The lobby of the Bentick Hotel
(A Monday afternoon in early October. 12 Noon.)

(Sound: country music)

(The MAID sings with the music from the radio as she sweeps the carpet. After a moment, the DESK CLERK enters and changes station to an "easy listening" sound.
The MAID exits. VALERIE, who is sitting on a chair near the entrance door of the hotel, rises and crosses to DESK CLERK. VALERIE is a young-looking 53-year-old woman.
The DESK CLERK lights her cigarette; it is an habitual, friendly moment. VALERIE smiles her thank you and returns to her chair. The DESK CLERK studies his racing form.)

(D enters. She is a 35-year-old woman filled with excitement and expectation. She looks around hotel lobby and sees VALERIE. D looks at VALERIE carefully, wondering if she will say hello to her. VALERIE looks at D and opens the book in her lap and reads. D looks to see if there is anyone else waiting in the lobby, sees that there isn't, and stands in thought next to the reception counter, unaware of the DESK CLERK behind her.)

DESK CLERK: Yes?

D: Oh. Nothing. Sorry. Thank you. *(She points to clock.)* It's only twelve. Thank you. *(She whispers to DESK CLERK. She refers to VALERIE.)* How long has she been here?

DESK CLERK: Fourteen years.

D: Fourteen years?

DESK CLERK: Been meeting the same man in the lobby every Friday.

D: It's Monday.

DESK CLERK: Was when I got up. Meeting somebody?

D: Yes.

DESK CLERK: Have a seat.

(D *sits on settee. She folds her coat, places it on the seat beside her, sneaks her brush out of her bag and straightens her hair, removes a large-sized bag of M and M's, squeezes bag to find there isn't even one left. She speaks softly to the* DESK CLERK, *who is reading his racing form*)

D: Excuse me. Excuse me. Do you have a cigarette machine?

DESK CLERK: Machine's broken.

(*The* MAID *enters, carrying a cleaning bucket.*)

D: A candy machine?

MAID: It's all right, honey. Someone left some. (*She takes a pack of opened cigarettes out of pail.*) Menthols.
(*To* DESK CLERK) From Room 506.

(*The* MAID *and* DESK CLERK *laugh at their private joke.* D *returns pack of cigarettes.*)

D: Thanks. No. I quit months ago. I think. And I really don't need candy. I have toothpicks which, since they always disintegrate in my mouth, I consider a type of food. (*She refers to* VALERIE.) That can't be her. She's too young, right?

DESK CLERK: Pardon?

D: I'm sorry. I'm being manic. And I'm very aware of it. But I do think I was a little bit more articulate when I smoked.

DESK CLERK: Have a seat.

D: Thank you. (*She sits on settee.*)

(*Lights dim on hotel.*)

(Lights up on D.)

PLACE: D's fantasy

(D speaks to audience.)

D: A funny thing happened to me in the lobby of the Bentick Hotel. I'd walked in to meet my real mother, who for this or that reason hadn't got around to meeting me yet, and she was in disguise as a Desk Clerk. A terrific disguise. She took one look at me and said: Have a seat. It made perfect sense. She had to check me out first. I mean, what would you do if somebody called you and said: Hey, remember me? We met once 35 years ago. I'm your daughter. The one you gave up for adoption. *(A dog barks on street.)* What if my real mother was Lassie? Can you imagine being Lassie's kid? Lying between her strong paws. The side of her mouth goes up when anyone tries to come near me. But there's a forest fire. And, in the confusion, we get separated. And, before she can get to me, a kind, human family adopts me and are very good to me and, of course, I take on their mannerisms. But 35 years later, in Boston, Lassie walks by the Bentick. She stops, tenses, sniffs the air. Knows I'm in here the way only a mother knows her own. And she breaks down the door. Kisses me, licks me, rolls me on the floor. But we have to stop. This is a hotel. So I say: Momma. Sit. Momma. Heel. Momma. Stay! *(With emotion to the mother who left her)* Momma. Stay.

(The hotel phone rings.)

(Lights up on hotel.)

(D runs to phone and answers it.)

D: Hello.... *(To* DESK CLERK*)* Sorry. It's for the hotel. *(She hands phone to* DESK CLERK.*)* Sorry. I have this thing about phones.

(D gives phone to DESK CLERK.*)*

(Lights dim on hotel.)

(Lights up on D.)

PLACE: D's fantasy

D: *(To herself)* Slow, D. Go slow. Slow. *(She calms herself, then speaks to audience as she relives her phone call to her real mother.)*

D: I spoke to her two days ago. I heard my real mother's voice. I dialed the phone and she said "Hello." That's her voice. "Hello." I never imagined that would be her voice. It so threw me, I couldn't remember my name. Which started me off into a routine about how I should know my name after 35 years. And she said: May I help you? I'm sure she meant the polite "May I help you?" But I swear it sounded like she wanted to help me. And I said: "All I know is that I was born February 7, 1954 and did she think she knew me? " And she said: "Yes. She did." And I'm here! I'm meeting her in the lobby of the Bentick Hotel in Boston at 12:15. I'm here.... What's so ironic is that it was also a phone call. An everyday, ordinary phone call. That started me here. Started my search.

(LEAH enters. She crosses into her area and lifts her phone off the hook.)

(The phone rings in D and MICHAEL's area.)

(D moves to answer her phone as she finishes telling her story to audience.)

D: In another lifetime.

(Phone rings.)

(MICHAEL's voice, off-stage)

MICHAEL: D.

(D sits at her desk and lets phone ring as she looks for a cigarette.)

D: *(To audience)* A year and a half ago.

(Phone rings.)

MICHAEL: *(Offstage)* The phone.

D: *(To audience)* When all I wanted was a smoke.

PLACE: A corner of D's home,
a corner of LEAH's home

(MICHAEL enters. He is D's husband, a nurturing and caring man.)

MICHAEL: D. The phone.

D: I know. I know. It's my mother.

(She takes a deep inhale and answers phone.)

(MICHAEL pulls cookbook from shelf and rechecks a recipe he is in the process of making in the off-stage kitchen.)

(LEAH, D's adoptive mother, a 65-year-old woman, born in Poland, fully at home with the English language, but retaining her European manner, waits for D to answer phone.)

D: *(Picking up phone)* Hi. Sorry. I was in the kitchen.

LEAH: Are you all right, Dorothy?

D: Hundred percent.

LEAH: You still not smoking? This is three days, right?

D: Right. *(She blows smoke away from phone.)* Did the landlord fix the leak?

LEAH: I have to call him. Three days! I knew you could stop. So. *(LEAH uses 'so' as a closure to a spoken or unspoken thought.)* Do you have a minute?

D: Sure. *(D holds receiver upside down, with mouthpiece by her hair, so that LEAH won't hear her smoking.)*

LEAH: I have a story for you. I was at the bus stop yesterday, and I talked to a woman who told me she had just lost a kidney. And we had such a conversation about loss, survival, and hope. The most philosophical conversation I had in years. But when she got on her bus and the bus pulled out, I realized, she'd been talking about having lost a kitten. Little ears. Little tail. A kitten! I couldn't stop laughing.

(D enjoys her mother's stories. She laughs fully, which causes her to cough.)

D: *(Coughing)* A kitten....*(She coughs harder.)*

LEAH: Dorothy?

D: *(Coughing)* I'm fine.

LEAH: Are you smoking?

D: No. Yes. But please let's not talk about smoking. Not everyone can give up smoking.

LEAH: I didn't call about smoking. And you know as well as me if you plan to have a baby you shouldn't smoke.

D: Mother, please let's not talk about babies. Michael and I are not planning to have a baby.

LEAH: Yes, but no one knows when they are going to have a baby.

D: We know because we're not planning to have one.

LEAH: That's not what I'm saying. I'm saying no one knows exactly when they are going to have a baby....

D: Mother....

LEAH: So when a woman is smoking at the time she gets pregnant....

D: Mother....

LEAH: Since no one knows the exact moment of conception....

D: Didn't I ask you....

LEAH: Because it's in the first three weeks of pregnancy....

(D screams.)

LEAH: What?

D: Oh my God. A pigeon flew in the room.

LEAH: A pigeon?

(D sits calmly in chair, using only her voice to create the imaginary pigeon crisis.)

D: Oh God, it's on the desk! *(She calls as though* MICHAEL *weren't in room.)* Michael. Michael!

LEAH: A pigeon?

D: I'll call you tomorrow. Okay. Bye. *(D hangs up quickly.)*

(Lights dim on LEAH.*)*

MICHAEL: A pigeon?

D: That's all I could think of. Next time she starts, I'll tell her. It's not me. It's the stork. The stork won't give me a baby.

MICHAEL: Why not?

D: *(Improvises)* Because he can't find me. I'm not registered. I don't have a birth certificate. So what are you going to teach me to cook tonight?

MICHAEL: Why don't you write for your birth certificate?

D: *(As a Cabbage Patch doll)* Dear Sirs. I came from the Cabbage Patch Factory and what do you know? You forgot to put my certificate in the box.

*(*MICHAEL *ignores her. In Spanish:)*

MICHAEL: Pendeja.

D: But seriously, folks. Have you ever seen a doll uglier than a Cabbage Patch Doll? Those dolls were so ugly they had to be adopted.

MICHAEL: What do you want me to do when you get like this?

D: My real mother was a stand-up comic. It's in my genes.

MICHAEL: Are you going to do it or not?

D: Do what?

MICHAEL: Write for your birth certificate.

D: If I do it, it's nothing to do with wanting a baby.

MICHAEL: Did I say that? *(After a beat, D goes to desk. She finds writing paper. She realizes the possible consequences of her action and controls her fear. She turns back to MICHAEL.)*

D: I'm not going on any search. I'm not reading the other parts. I'm not reading my mother and father's names.

MICHAEL: How can you not want to know who your mother and father are?

D: All I want is my name.

(MICHAEL exits.)

(D writes for a beat.)

(Lights in D's home dim.)

PLACE: D's fantasy

(D turns in chair and speaks to audience with an English accent.)

D: Actually, it was a choice between two names.
My mum and I... my real mother spent her pregnancy reading Jane Austen, looking for names for me.
And when she found a good one, she'd tell me and I'd kick. One kick for no. Two kicks for yes.... My mother was a Rothschild. One of the English Rothschilds. They have their illegitimate babies in America....I would have been named Marianne Dashwood, but when she asked me if I liked it, I liked it so much I kicked too hard. And she said: "Your behavior is not good enough. It's just not good enough". So she named me....

(D stays in a moment of thought.)

(MICHAEL's voice is heard.)

MICHAEL: D. The mail.

(Lights up on D's home.)

(MICHAEL excitedly enters with letter.)

D: For me?

MICHAEL: Yes.

(The moment is overwhelming. D can't open letter.)

D: You read it. Please. Only the name. *(D looks for cigarette as* MICHAEL *opens and reads letter.)* How can I have no cigarettes?

MICHAEL: Oh for Christ's sake. *(He reads.)*
The information requested is stamped sealed. Your birth certificate can be opened only by a court order for a reason deemed good cause.

D: What does that mean?

MICHAEL: You are not allowed your birth certificate.

D: Allowed?

MICHAEL: You need a court order.

D: A court order for a birth certificate? Why am I not a good cause?

MICHAEL: Could Leah have it?

D: I don't know.

MICHAEL: You never asked her for your birth certificate?

D: No.

MICHAEL: You never did? That's square one.
(He lifts phone receiver.) Ask her.

D: We're seeing her tonight.

MICHAEL: You can still call her.

D: I can go over to her.

MICHAEL: You can call her now.

D: For God's sake, will you please let me handle this. I'm going over to her. *(MICHAEL looks at her disbelievingly. D gathers her courage.)* Okay. Now.

(Lights up on LEAH's *home.)*

(LEAH sits in her chair, knitting.)

(D walks toward LEAH's *area.)*

(She stops.)

PLACE: D's fantasy

D: (*To audience*) A funny thing happened to me on my way to my mother's. A woman, about 70, comes up behind me and says: "D Cruz?" I say: "Yes." And she cries. I say: "Can I help you? Are you lost? This is 98th Street." She says: "Please forgive me. I was waiting for you. You know me?" She looked me right in the eye and said she knew me. (*D becomes immersed in fantasy and does not act for the audience.*) I'm sorry. I didn't get your name. (*As woman*) Julia. Julia Brigham. (*As D, to woman*) Brigham's? I used to go to Brigham's in Newton for hot fudge sundaes....She walks closer to me. Soft white hair under her hat. And says: "I know you may not want to see me. I have no right to ask anything of you.
I have found you. You are...big." (*As D*) I'm 35.
She touches my hand. (*As woman*) You were the smallest in the hospital. (*As D, with wonder*)
"You've been looking for me?"

(*D turns and looks at* LEAH *knitting. She turns back to her fantasy and speaks with passion to the fantasy mother who would take her away from* LEAH)

D: Get out. Don't go near her. She's old. Don't hurt her. Get out of here!

(*The fantasy is over.* D *turns to enter* LEAH's *home. She is afraid to ask* LEAH *for the certificate and does not go in. On her way into present time and the hotel lobby,* D *passes* MICHAEL *at their desk. She stops and speaks to him.*)

D: I asked her. She doesn't have it.

(*She crosses into lobby.*)

PLACE: The hotel lobby

(*Lights: the present*)

(*The lobby phone rings.*)

DESK CLERK: (*Answering phone*) The Bentick. No. She's gone for the day. (*He hangs up phone and speaks to* D.) Did you give your people a call?

D: No.

DESK CLERK: Maybe it's the weather. The traffic.
What's that...? *(He finds phrase.)* Rain ends many a picnic.

*(D walks to phone, then turns from it, deciding not to call.
She sits in chair by phone)*

(Music: Richard Strauss's Zueignung*)*

(Lights dim on hotel lobby.)

PLACE: D and MICHAEL's home

*(LEAH and MICHAEL are enjoying their once-a-week
musicale evening. They "conduct" the music. D watches
from her hotel chair.)*

LEAH: It's too beautiful.

MICHAEL: Wait. Wait till you hear Fischer-Dieskau do it.

LEAH: I heard Jessye Norman on NCN. We must hear
her together.

MICHAEL: First Dieskau. His first "habe dank" is quiet,
quick. And the last! I get goose bumps. Do you think
anyone has ever danced to Richard Strauss's lieder?

LEAH: Rosenkavalier, yes. But a lied?

(MICHAEL offers his hand.)

MICHAEL: Madame.

(They dance.)

LEAH: *(While dancing)* I heard Della Casa in Boston. Her
voice was clear.

MICHAEL: Dieskau, Leah, Dieskau. Dieskau
understands a young man's 'thank you'. Strauss wrote
this when he was 18. *(He sings with emotion.)* "Habe
dank!"

LEAH: Yes. But Strauss could also write....

(She hums the opening bars of Meinem Kinde.*)*

*(D rises from chair and crosses through her home. LEAH
stops humming.)*

D: Don't stop. I have to be up at six. 'Night.

LEAH: *(To* MICHAEL*)* It is late.

*(*MICHAEL *and* LEAH *exit.)*

D: *(To audience)* Every time I walk in the room she's playing Strauss! And you don't have to say it. I know it. Everything isn't about you, D. Mother likes Strauss and her reason for liking Strauss is not because I was adopted from the Strauss Agency in Boston. It has nothing to do with me!

D: *(To God)* Help me. Help me see things outside of myself. Get me beyond the goddamn limitations of myself.... I know I have no right to you. I don't go to temple. I don't follow the laws. I don't know how to pray. But please help me. Let me say it once. Out loud. Say it for me. Not for Michael. Not for Leah. Just say once, out loud, that I do want a baby. *(To God)* Scratch that. Don't tell anyone. I didn't say it. *(To herself)* I can't be a mother. What if I'm like my real mother? What if I...? *(To God)* Please don't let me ever get pregnant unless I know who she is. *(She stands quietly for a beat, then crosses to* MICHAEL*, who sits at desk.)* Michael. I want to find her. I want to find my mother.

MICHAEL: *(With excitement)* We'll find her.

D: Yes?!

MICHAEL: Yes. We'll drive to Boston. Go to the adoption agency and see the director.

D: The director?

MICHAEL: They have a complete file on you. They have an answer for every one of your questions. They have information down to your mother's blood type. *(He writes on a pad.)*

D: They have?

MICHAEL: But those people don't slouch, and I know you with authority figures. You have to go there with your questions written down and with you.

(MICHAEL *hands her her list of questions.*)

D: Yes.

PLACE: The Strauss Agency in Boston

(MRS. JOHNSON, *the director of the agency, enters.*
She holds D's file and reads her name off top of file)

MRS JOHNSON: Dorothy Gartner. I'm Mrs. Johnson.
This needn't take long.

D: I'm D Cruz. My husband Michael. I'm interested in....

MRS JOHNSON: Before you begin, I'd best explain.
We at the Strauss Agency consider adoption a serious
commitment, and, in a moral and spiritual sense,
as sacred as marriage.

D: Yes, of course.

MRS JOHNSON: We are a child placement agency.
Our only concern is have we chosen the right parents
for the child.

D: Yes.

MICHAEL: D. Your questions.

MRS JOHNSON: I think your wife understands that her
adoption was a legal rebirth. An adoptable child is one
who has been legally surrendered.

MICHAEL: Ask her.

D: I....

MRS JOHNSON: I don't think you understand. A contract
was signed. Signed by your biological mother.

D: Yes. Of course.

MICHAEL: You have a right to her name.

MRS JOHNSON: We are legally bound to preserve....

MICHAEL: You have a right to your father's name....

MRS JOHNSON: If you can't control yourself, Mr Cruz,
I will leave the room.

MICHAEL: You have a right to this information.
A right to know what hospital you were born in....

MRS JOHNSON: We are legally bound to preserve that contract in strictest secrecy. You do understand.

MICHAEL: She has a right to know if she has sisters, brothers, aunts, nieces. A right to her grandfather....

MRS JOHNSON: Mr Cruz, if you do not leave now, I will leave now and your wife's appointment will be over.

(MICHAEL *exits and turns to* D.)

MICHAEL: You can't just stand there and nod and smile. *(He exits.)*

MRS JOHNSON: It's the law, Mrs Cruz. There's nothing you can do. It's the law.

D: *(Defeated)* Yes.

(D *folds her list into the smallest squares.* MRS JOHNSON *opens file, scanning over pages of information she cannot reveal.)*

MRS JOHNSON: What I can tell you is that you were born February 7, 1954, in Boston.

D: I know that.

(MRS JOHNSON *scans through files.)*

MRS JOHNSON: I cannot, of course, tell you the hospital. There is no record of your father. Your mother's parents had unobjectionable health records. She was 17 when she had you....

D: 17.

MRS JOHNSON: She was from Newton, Massachusetts. No. I meant, of course, you were placed in Newton, Massachusetts, with the Gartners. Leah and Howard. That's all we can tell you. Anything else you want to know?

(D *shakes head.)*

MRS JOHNSON: Your follow-up shows that Mr Gartner passed away. I'm sorry. Did your mother move to New York to be close to you? *(D nods.)* Think deeply on

why you want this information, Mrs Cruz. I hope you
have a nice drive back.

(MRS JOHNSON *exits.*)

(D *picks up a potted plant and crosses to* LEAH's *home.*)
                    PLACE: LEAH's home
(LEAH *is knitting a sweater for D. The front is nearly
completed. D enters.*)

LEAH: Was the drive nice?

D: (*Giving* LEAH *plant*) For you.

LEAH: Thank you. You always bring me the best plants.
(*She puts plant on window sill, next to others.*) What was it
like in Boston today?

(D, *uncomfortable with her lie, moves away.*)

D: Colder.

LEAH: Our winters were always colder in Newton. And
only twenty minutes from Boston. (LEAH *brings knitting
to* D.) Why do you stand there? (*She puts sweater against*
D.) Turn. (D *faces* LEAH.) So. Who did you see in Boston?

D: A friend from high school. She's going to help
Michael with some research for a book he's doing.

LEAH: What book?

D: A new book.

LEAH: Do I know this friend from high school?

(D *turns from* LEAH.)

D: The leak's not fixed.

LEAH: I keep a plant under it.

D: Did you see the landlord? What did he say?

LEAH: Like last time. I waited an hour and all he would
say is "Thank you for coming. I know about it."

D: What kind of information is that?

LEAH: I only know what he tells me.

D: And what did you do?

LEAH: What?

(In an irrational burst, D lets out her anger at herself for her own behavior in the agency office.)

D: Did you say yes, and nod and smile, and nod and smile?

LEAH: I don't....

D: You pay him. You have a right to his time. A right to his information. A right to have it fixed. This is your home. You can't keep sitting in offices like a good girl. You're 65 years old. It drives me crazy thinking you are nodding and smiling and nodding and smiling.

LEAH: Why do you...? *(She turns her face from D.)*

(D runs to her.)

D: I'm so sorry. *(She is in tears herself.)* Someday. I promise. I'm not going to make you cry.

(The two women comfort each other.)

LEAH: It was a long day.

D: It was. *(D gets a pad and pencil.)* You and I...we are going to sit down together and write a list of questions you want the landlord to answer. No one should go to a landlord's office without questions written down and with them.

LEAH: Yes.

D: He's going to answer you today on the phone.

LEAH: He doesn't talk on the phone.

(D puts her arms around LEAH.)

D: He's going to because I'm going to be standing next to you.

LEAH: Thank you.

(D stands behind the seated LEAH, her hands on LEAH's shoulders.)

(In the hotel lobby, VALERIE crosses to the DESK CLERK. Hotel music plays. D watches as the DESK CLERK lights

VALERIE's *cigarette. As* VALERIE *returns to her chair,*
D *leaves* LEAH.)

D: *(To herself)* She was seventeen.

PLACE: D's fantasy

(D *is a southern backwoods woman. Her fantasy mother, who
speaks to audience, enjoys telling them about* D's *birth.)*

D: I was seventeen and you came early. A month early.
Frankie and I were having a steak dinner. If you'd been
born an hour earlier, you'd have been born on Frankie's
birthday. That's why we were having steak. I thought I
was having indigestion. The steak was tough. I didn't
know what labor pains were. I got to the hospital an
hour before you came. The good thing I can say is that
you came out quick. But I never felt anything like you
coming out. They said "Push. Push." And I couldn't tell
the difference between pushing you out and going to
the bathroom. *(She giggles.)* I kept telling them to stop
telling me to push. I wasn't going to mess up their table.
And the pain got harder. Soon I couldn't hear the
nurses. Couldn't hear the doctor. I could only hear
myself shouting "I'm shitting on your table. I'm shitting
on your table." And then I heard you cry. And the
doctor pulled you out and a cord was hanging from
you. *(She laughs.)* I thought it was the thinnest, ugliest
cock I ever saw. I was going to call you Frankie Junior
to serve him right. But you were a girl. I could trace
Frankie down for you if you want to see him.
And I'll bet you ten to one, he's in some state pen doing
time for rape. Anything else you want to know?

(D, *frightened by her fantasy, as though she were woken from
a bad dream, calls for* MICHAEL.)

D: Michael. *(She runs to* MICHAEL.)

(MICHAEL *holds* D.)

MICHAEL: All you know is she was 17.

(She brings herself to reality.)

D: All I know is she was 17. 17 in Boston. I was 17 in Newton. 17 in my senior year. 17, getting good marks. And when she was 17, she was having me.
(With a smile) Ask me how old my mother was when she had me.

MICHAEL: How old was your mother when she had you?

(D enjoys the first piece of information she can tell about her mother.)

D: She was 17.

(A MAN, a member of the adoptee search group, Journey, crosses the stage, followed by LORRAINE. They establish the "Journey meeting area".)

(D and MICHAEL continue their scene in their home simultaneously.)

MAN: *(To audience)* Welcome to this evening's searchers' meeting. Our speaker tonight is Lorraine Hays-Williams.

(D moves away from MICHAEL, toward meeting area.)

MICHAEL: I thought you were going to learn chess tonight.

D: I'm going to a searchers' meeting.

MICHAEL: Okay! I'll get my coat.

D: No.

MAN: *(To audience)* The place to find your name is in your adoption papers.

D: *(To MICHAEL)* It's only for adoptees.

MAN: But never let people you want information from know you're an adoptee.

MICHAEL: Then go.

MAN: To them you're an adopted child, no matter how old you are. And they'll tell you nothing.

D: I'm sorry. (D *runs into Journey meeting area, pulling in a chair for herself. She apologizes for her lateness.*) I'm sorry.

MAN: *(To D)* And in conclusion, don't preface everything with 'sorry'. It gives you away as an adoptee. Lorraine.

PLACE: Journey meeting

(LORRAINE, *the main speaker, includes the audience as members of the searchers' group*)

LORRAINE: As most of you know, the hospital where I was born wouldn't give me my records and the doctor who delivered me was dead. But I was luckier than most of you, I got my mother's name. I was flying! Francine Williams somewhere in Milwaukee. I could only get a week off from work so on my way back to New York I stole a phone book. Williams! You can imagine how many. I didn't care. But it adds up calling from New York, so I could only do five a week. And I got one! A woman answered and said "YES." She knew Francine Williams ages ago. Sure she remembered her because they had the same last name, worked in the same supermarket. And, she also remembered her because she had the most beautiful fingernails. I could hardly hold myself down. I asked did she know where she was now? And she said she'd moved to Georgia when she got married.

(LORRAINE *relives the phone conversation in detail, portraying the other woman's voice, etc.*)

LORRAINE: Did she know where in Georgia? Atlanta. Did she remember her husband's last name? No. He was a short white man. And I knew it right away! My mother gave me up for adoption because she fell in love with a short white liberal, who worked for the civil rights movement, and travelled alot, because he marched with Dr King. And my mother marched with Dr King! So I asked the woman to please please try to remember Francine's married name. And she said,

"Oh honey, how can I remember two honkies from over
20 years ago?" Now, the one thing all my certificates say
is race: Black. So I asked her what shade Francine was?
Could she pass for black? She said, "Oh, that girl was as
white as Snow White." And I said "Well, how white is
that!" And she hung up, leaving the phone off the hook.
That should have been it, right? But when all you have
is the smallest piece of your life, it's hard to let go of
any clue...wrong or right. *(She laughs.)* Rose and I sat
up, with Rose saying over and over, "You look black,
Lorraine." And I took off my clothes and we inspected
this blackness.... It took the whole night for me to say it
was the wrong Francine and I wasn't white. But I'm still
calling. *(She gestures to D to introduce herself.)*

D: *(Stands)* I'm D Cruz. This is my first meeting.
I edit gothic romances written by Texas men wearing
women's names. Do you want to know that?
I'm going to start my search tomorrow. (The MAN *gives
her a booklet.)* This is very exciting. Thank you.

(LORRAINE *hugs* D. *The* MAN *returns the chairs to position.*
D *runs to* MICHAEL.)

PLACE: D's home

(MICHAEL *is sitting at desk with a half-eaten loaf of Wonder
Bread beside him.* D *runs in excitedly.)*

D: I said I was searching. This is the searchers'
handbook. I feel like I've joined a secret underground.
I'm going to ask Leah for my birth records tomorrow.
My birth name's in them.

MICHAEL: I waste too much of my life figuring out how
to say things to you.

D: I wanted you to come. Closed meetings is their
policy.

MICHAEL: This is not about the meeting.

D: I know the feeling of not being allowed in.
In high school....

MICHAEL: This is about me. I'm decompensating.
I'm eating Wonder Bread. I'm doing it again.
Asking myself "Where's my novel?" At 35, I'm a writer,
I should have a novel. I don't need a novel. I don't have
the ego for fiction. I write about how to fix things
because I like to fix things. So what am I doing sitting
here, needing? And it's physical. It's crazy.
Like a full moon moving through me. And, finally, I let
myself understand. It's needing a kid. I know how you
feel. I know we agreed we might not have one.
But I can't keep on not saying things to you.

D: Then we...I won't. I won't start again tomorrow.
I won't take the pill anymore.

*(Both take a moment to understand what they have said to
each other. D lightens the moment for herself by attempting
to tease MICHAEL in Spanish, which she mispronounces.)*

D: Pendayo.

MICHAEL: *(Correcting)* Pendejo.

D: Pendejo. Pendejo. It makes me feel like my great
grandmother came from Madrid and my grandmother
from...?

*(MICHAEL tells her where his grandmother comes from,
while speaking Spanish to her, which D loves for him to do.)*

MICHAEL: San German. Diez y siete Calle Christo.
Mantiene la apariencia de un pequeño pueblo español
con aire de culture.

D: Con aire de culture.

*(They kiss. After a full beat of lovemaking, D turns her head
away.)*

MICHAEL: What is it? Your papers? *(D nods.)*
That's tomorrow.

D: Would you sing?

MICHAEL: "Come to me my melancholy baby."

D: Tell me you want me.

MICHAEL: *(Sings)* Baby. I want. Want. Want you.

D: *(Laughing)* It's sick to need that.

MICHAEL: I want you.

(A beat of lovemaking)

D: Please don't let me stop myself.

MICHAEL: I won't let you.

(MICHAEL takes off D's coat, letting it drop on floor as they exit.)

PLACE: LEAH's home

(Lights up on LEAH turning on radio.)

(Participants of a radio talk show—DR CROYERS and her caller, DANNY—enter and stand at side of stage.)

DOCTOR: Hello, Danny. You're on the air with Dr Helen Croyers.

DANNY: Hello. I'd like to speak to....

DOCTOR: This is Dr Helen Croyers, Danny.

(D enters, picks up her coat, puts the coat on, and crosses into LEAH's area.)

DANNY: Oh, Dr Croyers. I've listened to your program every afternoon since I've been home from the hospital and I think you're a wonderful person.

(D enters LEAH's room. LEAH hands her a folder and returns to 'actively' listening to the radio, to cover the emotion of the moment.)

D: My adoption papers?

(LEAH nods.)

DOCTOR: Thank you, Danny, and what is on your mind today that you would like to share?

(D holds folder, uncomfortable about opening it in front of LEAH.)

DANNY: My daughter keeps her coat on when she walks into the house.

DOCTOR: Yes. And how old is your daughter?

DANNY: Thirty-one. Thirty-two by now. I think about it all night. She doesn't take her coat off anymore, Doctor, when she comes to visit.

(D, *whose coat is on, turns to radio.*)

DOCTOR: Is it cold in the house, Danny?

DANNY: Oh no. I keep the thermostat at seventy-eight. I don't even need to wear pajamas.

(LEAH *laughs.*)

D: Do we need the radio on?

(LEAH *turns it off.*)

LEAH: No.

(DANNY *and the* DOCTOR *exit.*)

LEAH: Do you have what you want in there?

D: Thank you for finding them.

LEAH: They were in the cabinet. (*She reaches for her sewing box, then decides she doesn't want to sew.*)

(*There is a beat of silence. Neither woman knows how to start. After a beat, D moves closer to* LEAH. LEAH *stops her with her words, words she did not even know she was going to say.*)

LEAH: So. Tell Michael I don't know if I can come to hear music on Sundays anymore.

D: Oh?

LEAH: I'm going to start with the Red Cross. It might be Sundays.

D: That's good.

LEAH: That I don't come?

D: No. That you're with the Red Cross...volunteering again.

LEAH: Yes. They need people. So. You have to go now.

D: No.

LEAH: Is there ice on the streets?

D: It's all right on Broadway. Do you have to go out now?

LEAH: I don't know. If you're staying, I'll be here. If you're....

D: Mother. Do you have to go somewhere now?

LEAH: I don't have to go now.

D: I don't have to stay, if you're....

LEAH: You never stay long, so I thought if you were going out that I would.

D: I wasn't, but I can go if you're going out.

LEAH: Stay. I like it when you stay.

D: I want to stay.

(D *takes her coat off.* LEAH *removes a red wrap-around skirt she is making for D from the sewing basket.*)

LEAH: Come.

(D *holds box of straight pins as* LEAH *pins up the hem of skirt.*)

D: *(Gently)* Mother. I joined a group called Journey. It's for adoptees.

LEAH: *(Pinning skirt)* I heard about them on *The Phil Donahue Show.* They seem to be a very good group.

D: They are.

LEAH: And you go to meetings?

D: I've been to one.

LEAH: Nice people?

D: Yes. Very nice.

LEAH: *(Ending subject)* Good. You don't have to tell me. I heard about them.

(*After a beat of pinning and handing pins,* D *tries to open subject again.*)

D: Did you know my birth mother was 17?

LEAH: No.

D: Have you read the papers?

LEAH: I didn't ever read them. Is that what they say?

D: I don't know. I haven't looked in them yet.

LEAH: Why didn't you tell me that you wanted them?

(There is a silent beat.)

D: I have to get to the store before Michael gets home. You going down too?

LEAH: I'm not a mountain goat anymore.

D: I'll take you over the curbs.

LEAH: I don't want to go out.

D: I'll let myself out.

(D exits LEAH's area. She stands and opens her file. She reads from the papers.)

D: Dana. Dana Tannenbaum. I am Dana Tannenbaum.

(MICHAEL enters, singing.)

MICHAEL: O tannenbaum. O tannenbaum. Wie schoen sind deine blette....

D: *(Laughs)* Oh, what if I was baptized before I was adopted and I'm a German Catholic who is now a Jew without having told the rabbi that I'm Catholic? I'm irretrievable.

MICHAEL: Join the rest of us.

(He crosses into their home area.)

(D stands in light.)

D: *(Looking at papers)* Dana. Why Dana?

PLACE: D's fantasy

(D fantasizes about the conversation between her real mother and grandmother. She plays both roles, using her coat as the baby.)

THE 17-YEAR-OLD MOTHER: Why Dana? Why call her Dana, Momma? It's not a Jewish name, Momma.

THE GRANDMOTHER: A good Jewish girl would do what you did? Look at the baby. *(She sighs.)* Today I saw a rat.

THE 17-YEAR-OLD MOTHER: She looks like a rat?

THE GRANDMOTHER: What's over is over.
Write down Dana. D for your Uncle David.
May he never know this happened.

THE 17-YEAR-OLD MOTHER: Mama, she can hear!

THE GRANDMOTHER: If you say it softly all words are lullabies. *(She speaks softly.)* Rat. Rat. You look like a rat.

THE 17-YEAR-OLD MOTHER: Why'd you make me have it, Momma?

THE GRANDMOTHER: To go up to East Harlem and lie on a kitchen table? You wanted that? My bright girl! My honor-student girl! Says to herself: "It takes at least six months after you stop the pill to get pregnant." And what happened? Like a shiksa. Like the Virgin Mary, it happened the first time. Like you! What happened to you?

(D turns to MICHAEL.*)*

PLACE: D's home

D: I'm pregnant.

MICHAEL: I thought you said it took six months.

D: I thought it did.

MICHAEL: You are? I mean, you really are? *(D nods.)* Oh God, you really are. *(He throws his arms around her.)* Habe dank! Habe dank!

(D gets a leg cramp.)

D: I got a....

MICHAEL: Where? What? Is it the baby?

D: No. In my leg. Foot. The leg.

(MICHAEL pushes D's toes back to break the spasm. D yells in pain.)

MICHAEL: Push your toes back. Don't fight it.
Say tomato soup.

D: *(In pain)* Tomato soup.

MICHAEL: Keep on.

(D repeats "tomato soup." MICHAEL relieves spasm.)

MICHAEL: Leave it up for a minute....
(He embraces her stomach.) You're pregnant!

D: *(With mixed feelings)* Yeah. It's great. It's great.
But can I just have a week. Just one week not to tell
anyone. Just till I've seen Dr Prager.

MICHAEL: You didn't see him for the test?

D: I did. This appointment is for my records.
He can get my birth records for me.

MICHAEL: How can he get your birth records?

D: Any doctor can get them for you.

MICHAEL: You're kidding.

D: It's not strictly legal, but he can get them for me if I
can get him on my side. The problem is me.
What if I sit like a good girl and nod and smile.

MICHAEL: You practice. Sit here. *(MICHAEL pulls chair
into position for what will be the Doctor's Office.)*
What he might do. What he might say is...."Why, D?
Why? You've had good parents in Leah and Howard".

D: *(Slumps in chair)* I'm finished.

MICHAEL: No. You sit up straight. Come on. Straight.
And say: "Doctor. I'm not looking for new parents.
I'm looking for myself."

D: *(Impressed)* Hey.

*(MICHAEL twirls the desk chair in place for the DOCTOR and
exits as the DOCTOR enters.)*

PLACE: The DOCTOR's office
(The DOCTOR is proud of being an understanding man.)

DOCTOR: I can't think of anyone who doesn't have ambivalent feelings towards their parents.
Everyone at one time wished they had others.
Myrna Loy and William Powell were mine.

D: I'm 35, Dr Prager. I'm not looking for new parents. I'm looking for myself.

DOCTOR: I know. How's Leah?

D: Leah?

DOCTOR: She hasn't been in. It must be a year.

D: I guess she's fine.

DOCTOR: You don't speak to her?

D: I speak to her every day. I meant she must be fine if you haven't seen her. I see her.

DOCTOR: Yes. I know.

(D *shows* DOCTOR *the letter.*)

D: For the purposes of this letter, I'm not D Cruz but Dana Tannenbaum. That's my real name.
And all the letter says is *(She reads.)* "Dana Tannenbaum is my patient. Forward all records from February 7, 1954 to today." That's all. You only have to sign it.

(D *gives* DOCTOR *the letter.*)

D: And I'll copy it and send it to every hospital in Boston. The one I was born in will send you my birth records and you'll give them to me. Then I'll have the names and addresses of my mother, my father, my grandparents.

DOCTOR: I know all about it. But what you want is information that the law...not I...the law has sealed.

D: But you can get it for me.

DOCTOR: Is Leah tickled about her first grandchild?

D: She doesn't know yet. *(The* DOCTOR *looks up from letter.)* I don't believe in telling till the third month.

DOCTOR: She doesn't know?

D: Doctor Prager, we were talking about the letter.

DOCTOR: Let's be open. You're not asking me to sign this letter for medical reasons.

D: I never told you about my allergy. I'm near a cat and in two minutes I can't breathe. Where did that come from?

DOCTOR: I'm a gynecologist. I've known you and Leah since you both....

D: Why do you keep throwing Leah into this?

DOCTOR: To be direct, D, you were fortunate to have parents.

D: I was white, healthy, and Jewish.

DOCTOR: You have to understand. You're my patient. Leah's my patient. I see so much of her in you.

D: But my baby won't look like her. She might look like me. She's going to be the first member of my family that I'm going to know. (D *pleads openly to the* DOCTOR, *letting her emotion show.*) I don't want to stare at her face, like I stare at my own, looking for clues. I don't want to find out from her what diseases are in my family. I don't want to be this afraid of having her.

DOCTOR: I know. I know what you're experiencing.

D: You don't know. You don't know what it's like to be cut off at birth. To live in fantasy. To know nothing except what you make up yourself. I need simple, basic information. Please give me that information. So I can give her a chance. So I can give her myself.

DOCTOR: I'd like to. But I'm responsible to many people. I can't break the law.

(*The* DOCTOR *exits.*)

(D *tears up letter.*)

D: I don't need you (*She gets an idea.*) I don't even need your name. I have made up more names, more mothers, more love stories, more rapes than you have patients

out there. (*She enjoys her decision.*) I can make up one more name: Dr Marianne Dashwood. I'll have fancy stationery and I'll write to the hospitals myself. Because screw being a good girl so I won't get sent back. Because it's a crock. Because it's nuts.
Because all those years I was so afraid of being sent back, nobody knew where to send me back to!

(D *sings happily to herself as she does the 'housekeeping' of putting the chairs back in their areas.*)

D: "Take it to the limit. Take it to the limit. Take it to the limit. One more time."

MICHAEL: (*Entering, with letters*) Dr Dashwood.

PLACE: D's home

(*In good spirits, D throws her arms around* MICHAEL.)

D: Thank you kind and noble patient or one of the noble and patient kind.

(*She drops letters after weighing them for heft.*)

D: More rejection slips.

MICHAEL: You can't be sure.

D: They're thin like the others. If my records were in them they'd be fat. (*She picks up letters.*)
These are rejection slips.

MICHAEL: They're not rejecting you. You weren't born in their hospital.

D: Which almost makes every hospital in Boston.

(*The phone rings.*)

(*Lights up in* LEAH's *home.*)

(LEAH *is waiting for* D's *phone to answer.*)

MICHAEL: Hello.

LEAH: Hello, Michael?

MICHAEL: Yes.

LEAH: Excuse my bothering you at home.
This is Leah Gartner speaking.

MICHAEL: I know it's you, Leah.

(On hearing it's LEAH, *D signals "no".)*

LEAH: Is Dorothy home? I keep missing her.
She seems so busy now. Is she there, please?

MICHAEL: One minute.

(He puts hand over receiver.)

D: I'm not here. Please. I'm not here.

MICHAEL: That's stupid. It's time you told her.

D: Please. Please. Please.

MICHAEL: *(Into phone)* Leah.

LEAH: Yes.

MICHAEL: She must have left. I had Strauss on.
I thought she was still here.

LEAH: Thank you.

MICHAEL: How are you feeling?

LEAH: Fine for winter.

MICHAEL: Well....I'll tell her you called. Bye.

LEAH: Bye.

*(*LEAH *and* MICHAEL *hang up phones.)*

(Lights off LEAH.*)*

MICHAEL: I'm never being a part of this again!

D: I can't do it all and not smoke at the same time.

MICHAEL: Do you know how that made me feel?

D: I'm sorry.

MICHAEL: When are you going to tell her?

D: I'm going to tell her.

MICHAEL: When?

D: When I know how.

MICHAEL: You say "I'm pregnant."

D: I will.

MICHAEL: She's home.

D: *(Opening a letter)* One thing at a time.

MICHAEL: She'd like to hear NOW.

D: I just told her I was searching. I can't throw everything at her.

MICHAEL: What are you throwing at her?

D: I can have a baby. She can't have a baby. Everything I'm doing. I feel like I'm leaving her.

MICHAEL: But this is for her. She always wanted us to have a baby.

D: I know she's not going to mind waiting.

MICHAEL: How do you know?

D: I know Leah.

MICHAEL: The people you know are the ones you make up.

(She stops him from exiting by taking his hand.)

D: I know you.... Why is it so important that I tell her now?

MICHAEL: Because I want to talk about the baby. Because I want to make a fool of myself. I want it real.

D: It is real. I'm having your baby.

MICHAEL: You're having my baby?

D: No. I didn't....

MICHAEL: If you don't want it, you say you don't want it. You don't say you're having it for me. 'Cause if that's all it is to you, you can give it to me. You walk out after you've had it and give it to me.

D: *(With force)* She's not something to give.

(MICHAEL exits.)

(After a beat, D dials the phone.)

(Phone rings in LEAH's area.)

(LEAH lifts phone. D responds quickly.)

D: I was out.

LEAH: I spoke to Michael.

D: He told me you called.

LEAH: He was listening to Strauss.

D: He likes him. So what do you think? I'm pregnant.

LEAH: You know? You know from a doctor?

D: Yes. And Dr Prager said you were to come in....

LEAH: *(Very happy)* Oh my Dorothy. Oh my Dorothy. *(She speaks in Polish.)* Dorotko!

(The warmth in LEAH's *voice allows* D *to feel a joy about her pregnancy that she has repressed in her guilt and fears.)*

D: Yeah. Yeah.

LEAH: Dorotko! Bocian wreszcie przynios dziecko. ("Dorothy! The stork finally brought the baby.")

D: Yeah. I'm pregnant!

LEAH: Oh my Dorothy, I will knit!

D: *(Smiling and crying)* Yes.

LEAH: Something that fits this time. With a little hat that goes with it.

D: And little feet at the end.

LEAH: Can I.... Can I come? Can we go together?

D: Yes.

LEAH: We will go together for a little bed. Oh my Dorothy.

D: We're going together.

LEAH: Oh Dorotko jaka ja jestem szcesliwa.... ("Oh little Dorothy how I am happy.")

(In her happiness, D throws the letters from the hospitals into the trash can.)

D: She's dead!

LEAH: Who is dead?

D: My mother. She died at St. Dominic's. I got the letter from the hospital. I'm not going to Boston anymore. There's the doorbell. I'll call you later. *(She quickly hangs up the phone.)*

(She takes a beat to understand what has just happened.)

D: *(To herself)* It's over.

(LORRAINE *enters.)*

LORRAINE: Get a Boston yellow pages. Find which hospitals were open then but are closed now.

D: No more. I'm not searching anymore.

(D *crosses into hotel.)*

PLACE: Hotel lobby

(D *walks past* DESK CLERK *to get her coat.)*

D: I'm going home.

DESK CLERK: What do you want me to tell her if she comes?

(His question stops D.)

(Realistic lights dim.)

D: *(To herself)* I don't need her. I have a mother.

PLACE: Fantasy, the past

(D *looks at* LEAH.)

D: Tell me, Momma. Tell it to me again.

(LEAH rises and speaks to D as if she were six years old. She holds a pin made of pearls.)

LEAH: Once upon our time I lost this pin. These are two magic circles of perfect pearls and each pearl has a story to tell. My grandmother and her mother had worn it, and my mother gave it to me when I was 21. And one year before you came to me, I lost it. I looked and looked and cried and cried. But I had to stop crying and I did. But one day, a year later, all morning I thought about the pin again. I was sad. And then at twelve noon, the phone rang, and it was the woman from the agency telling me that I was going to have the most

beautiful daughter coming to me on Monday. I ran to
your room and moved your bassinet into the sun and
put my hand in the warm spot where you were going
to lie, and I felt something under the blanket and it was
our pin.

(D *reaches her hand out for pin.* LEAH *holds it back, as from
a child.*)

LEAH: It will be yours when you are twenty-one and
you will give it to your daughter and she will give it to
hers. Two circles of perfect pearls joining all of us
together.

(*During the end of* LEAH's *story,* D *puts her head on her
mother's lap.* LEAH *strokes her hair.*)

(VALERIE *rises and crosses the stage. The* DESK CLERK
lights her cigarette. D *watches her from* LEAH's *lap.*
VALERIE *sits.* D, *torn between the two women, stands alone.*)

D: What if she came and she said: I loved you like Leah
did. I had no pearls. I had nothing but you. Let me tell
you how I loved you. You were my love child.
Say it with me. (D, *who has never been able to think of
herself as a loved child, refuses to acknowledge the thought.
With great difficulty, she allows the cathartic moment of
accepting that she could be loved.*) Say it. Love child.
Again. Love child. Say it. (*The release comes.*)
Love child...I want her.

(D *resumes search with energy. She crosses to* LORRAINE.)

D: Who do I call?

LORRAINE: I found one. Camden Hospital closed in '62.
When a hospital closes, its records are sent to some
insurance company in Boston.

(D *runs to her phone. She speaks to* MICHAEL, *who enters
with Boston yellow pages.*)

D: What's the next number?

MICHAEL: 976-3392.

D: *(Dialing)* Too many nines. It's not going to be this one. *(To* MICHAEL*)* M and M's? *(He shakes his head. To woman on phone:)* Hello. I'm Mrs Dashwood from Medical Insurance in New York. We're trying to locate the placement of the Camden Hospital records. It closed in '62. We're looking for the records of a Dana Tannenbaum. Yes, I can hold. *(To* MICHAEL*)* A toothpick? Anything?

MICHAEL: Stay with it.

D: *(To woman on phone)* Yes. *(She shouts.)* You have it! *(She hugs* MICHAEL *and screams. Then pulls herself back together.)* Sorry. It's my boss's birthday. We all had champagne. Yes, he's a wonderful boss. Yes. What we need is Dana's mother's name and address. *(*MICHAEL *writes down information as* D *receives it.)* Valerie Tannenbaum. 115 Pond Street. Her mother's name? Yes. Irmgard. Thank you. *(She hangs up. The depth of the moment is realized by both of them.)* We did it.

PLACE: In front of 115 Pond Street in Boston
(The OWNER *of house enters, wearing a Red Sox cap and holding a can of beer.)*

OWNER: I don't know any Tannenbaums.

*(*D *crosses to him and enters scene.)*

D: I know she lived in this house. 115 Pond Street.

OWNER: We bought it from the Turrelis, who moved to Bethesda.

D: Do you have their address?

OWNER: They're passed on.

D: Perhaps you could think of somebody who might know. You see, Tannenbaum's my aunt and her....

OWNER: If I can think of anything, I'll call you.

(He exits.)

*(*D *goes to pay phone.* MICHAEL *is at his phone.* LORRAINE *is at hers.)*

D: *(On phone)* I went to every house. I've said she looks like me. What if that's wrong? I can't say I don't know anything about her.

MICHAEL: *(On phone)* Find the family. Aunts. Uncles.

LORRAINE: *(On phone)* Go to the city records. Cross reference all the Tannenbaums from 1940 to 1954.

MICHAEL: *(On phone)* Stay with it. She has to be in Boston.

(LEAH *enters* MICHAEL's *area, overhearing his last words.*)

(D, *on the pay phone in Boston, looks up at a slide which appears on wall of set.*)

(Slide:
ARTHUR TANNENBAUM 1350 Commonwealth Ave
BEN TANNENBAUM 33 Williams Street
EUGENIA TANNENBAUM 1785 Mass Ave
JOEL TANNENBAUM 140 Franklin Street
JONATHAN TANNENBAUM 58 Cleveland Circle
LAWRENCE TANNENBAUM 18 Adams Street
RITA TANNENBAUM 3 Ogden Street
ROBERT TANNENBAUM 405 East Claremont Street

(D *stays at phone, in Boston, talking to Tannenbaums from slide.*)

(MICHAEL, *at their home in New York, sees* LEAH, *realizes she has overheard him, and hangs up phone.*)

D: Hello. Mr Arthur Tannenbaum? Hi. I'm a Tannenbaum too. I'm Valerie's daughter, Dana....

LEAH: Is Dorothy looking for her?

MICHAEL: Yes.

LEAH: She lied to me.

MICHAEL: *(Gently)* She's looking.

LEAH: Does she know the woman's name?

D: *(On phone)* Yes. I'm giving a surprise party for Valerie.

MICHAEL: Valerie.

LEAH: Valerie.

D: My grandmother was Irmgard.

LEAH: They lived in Boston?

D: We lived at 115 Pond Street.

MICHAEL: By the Fenway.

D: Oh. We're not related. Thank you so much.
(She dials another number from slide.)

LEAH: There's a nice museum there.

D: Hello. Jonathan Tannenbaum. Hi. I'm Dana
Tannenbaum. Valerie's daughter, Dana?

LEAH: She's coming back tonight?

MICHAEL: Yes.

D: Perhaps her mother, Irmgard....

LEAH: I don't want to hear music. Do you want to hear
music?

(MICHAEL shakes head. D hangs up and runs into room.)

D: It's not Tannenbaum. There's no Tannenbaum in
Boston.

(D sees LEAH.)

LEAH: I'll go home now. I'll call tomorrow.

(D goes to LEAH with an emotional apology)

D: I made up she was dead. I didn't want to find her.
But I....

LEAH: No. Conversations late at night never are what
we really mean to say. So we will both say goodnight.

D: No, don't go. Please tell me you understand.

LEAH: You are not a child. Don't ask my permission.

D: I'd like for you to stay. To tell me that you
understand.

(LEAH allows her emotion to come through.)

LEAH: You want my head. My intellect...I can say to you I understand. I understand you must go to her....
(Gently) It is late.

D: *(With difficulty)* I can't stop.

(There is a silent beat between the two women. LEAH exits.)

(LORRAINE enters. She leads D to the"Boston City Records Building".)

(D lifts a computer keyboard from behind counter. She types directions into computer. The computer "answers" as a MAN, who stands at the side of stage.)

LORRAINE: Tannenbaum is just a name. Names get screwed up. People mispronounce them. They turn into aliases. Let's play with Tannenbaum. Change the vowels.

(D types in names. The computer reads them.)

COMPUTER: A Thomas Tenebaum. 6 St Botolphs Street. Donald Tenebom. 70 Wallingford Street.

LORRAINE: Split them in two.

COMPUTER: Felix Tennen. 137 Foster Street. Joseph Tanens. 15 Alcott Street. Tanya Tanen. 24-25 Mulvey Street.

LORRAINE: Try the other half. It's got to go with 115 Pond Street.

COMPUTER: Jerry Baum. 59 Glenwood Avenue. Irmgard Baum. 115 Pond Street. Nathan Baum. Eustis Street.

D and LORRAINE: Go back. Go back. Wait. Go back!

(D carefully types in instructions.)

COMPUTER: Irmgard Baum. 115 Pond Street.

(D and LORRAINE scream, hug each other, jump up and down. LORRAINE controls them.)

LORRAINE: Let's get the records.

(D types in instructions as she speaks.)

D: Birth records for Irmgard or Valerie Baum.

COMPUTER: No record.

D: Marriage records for Irmgard or Valerie Baum.

COMPUTER: No record.

D: *(With fear)* Death records for Irmgard and Valerie Baum.

COMPUTER: No record.

(D places keyboard behind counter.)

D: My mother and grandmother were liars.
Paid their rent with one name and had me with another. They came to Boston and lied.

LORRAINE: If you had something of your father's.

D: I have nothing.

LORRAINE: You can't do anymore in Boston. Remember.
Remember anything anyone ever told you about her.
All you can do now is remember. *(She exits.)*

PLACE: D's fantasy/the past

(LEAH enters. D and LEAH act the memories without looking at each other. The first memory occurs when D is six years old.)

LEAH: She was too poor to keep you and her husband died in Korea.

D: Where is that? Am I Korean?

LEAH: He was American. We're all Americans.
He died in the Korean War before you were born.

D: Is she dead?

LEAH: Yes. She died in a plane crash.

D: Oh.

(LEAH crosses to indicate a new memory. D is fifteen years old.)

LEAH: We are going to Hawaii. You and Daddy and I.

D: I'm not going by plane.

LEAH: Dorothy. You're fifteen now.

D: My name is D, mother.

LEAH: D. This is our vacation. Daddy's worked hard. Everybody goes on planes.

D: I'll go by boat and railroad and bicycle and car and feet.

LEAH: She didn't die on a plane.

D: Is she alive?

LEAH: I don't know. We weren't allowed to know.

(MRS JOHNSON, *the agency director, enters.*)

MRS JOHNSON: What I can tell you is that you were born February 7, 1954 in Boston. I cannot, of course, tell you the hospital. There is no record of your father.
Your mother's parents had unobjectionable health records. She was 17 when she had you. She was from Newton, Massachusetts. No. I meant, of course....

D: I know. You told me.

(*She runs to* MICHAEL.)

PLACE: D's home

D: One call. Please. Only to Information. It's not Boston. It's Newton. 617. Where I grew up.

MICHAEL: It's not for me to do.

(*With fear and excitement, D dials Information.*)

D: (*On phone*) Yes. Newton....I'd like the number of a Valerie Baum or an Irmgard Baum, please....
You have both. Yes, I'd like both numbers.

(D *writes down numbers and places phone on receiver. There is a moment of silence.*)

D: She's real.

(D *has a physical reaction, a loss of breath.* MICHAEL *puts his hands on her shoulders. His touch quiets her.*)

MICHAEL: Yes. She's real.

(*After a beat, D stands.*)

D: I'll call from outside.

MICHAEL: I'll go in the bedroom.

D: I can't do it with everything I know around me.

(D exits her home and walks into LEAH's *area.)*

D: I found her.

LEAH: So. *(She stands and crosses to* D. *She lightly touches* D's *face and smoothes her hair: Her own silent and private goodbye.)* Yes...it is late now. *(Gently)* Go home.

(D crosses to center stage. She stands in thought, saying Leah's "so".)

D: So.

(She walks to pay phone, puts quarter to the slot.)

D: *(With wonder)* I'm calling her.

PLACE: Hotel lobby

(Lights up on D, *at phone, in present time.)*

(She angrily removes hand from slot and returns receiver to hook.)

D: I'm not calling that woman.

(VALERIE gets up from chair and crosses D's *path as she is about to exit.)*

VALERIE: Please, don't go.

(D looks at her.)

VALERIE: Hello.

(D takes a long beat, looking at VALERIE.)*

D: Hello.

END OF ACT ONE

ACT TWO

PLACE: The upstairs living room in VALERIE BAUM's house in Newton, Massachusetts

(The room is framed by the outline of a white Victorian two-storied house. There is a working door at the back wall which leads to the upstairs kitchen and bedrooms. The set has no side walls. A window through which we can see the time of day, the seasons, etc. hangs behind the couch. Three to six tied and filled laundry-type bags create a wall on one side of room.)

(At the side of the stage, the corner that had been LEAH's home in Act One, still contains LEAH's phone table, her chair, and her knitting.)

(The time moves from the present, an afternoon in December, into the past. The opening of Act Two takes place two months after the close of Act One.)

(D sits, in a spot light, on the couch, in the living room. She holds a letter.)

D: And then she drove me here.... A funny thing happened to me on my way to my mother's house. But seriously, folks, a funny thing happened to me on my way from the womb. I lost my mother, ran into her 35 years later, spent one afternoon with her. One. And she took one look at me and went to Australia. *(She looks at room and allows her emotion to come through.)* She left. She left and left me this house as a gift. *(She shows letter.)* Says it right here. Cross my heart and hope to die. *(The second emotion, her anger, comes out.)* I'm selling this house and everything in it.

(Full lights up)

(MICHAEL enters, carrying a large carton.)

MICHAEL: It's time. The movers want to do this room.

(D rises quickly.)

D: Please, five minutes. Please. I have to find something that will tell me why she left.

MICHAEL: Okay. But it's time.

(He exits.)

(D looks at room.)

D: The answer is in here. In this room. Her room.

(Lights change to an early October afternoon.)

VALERIE'S VOICE: Horace! Molly! Get down. Horace! Wait till I get my hands on you.

(D pulls out a wad of tissues from her pocket. She blows her nose, wipes her eyes, etc. She is having a severe allergy attack.)

D: Why didn't she tell me she had cats?

VALERIE'S VOICE: I'd like to remind you...and that's for you too, Horace. That you are cats. You don't own this house yet. Molly, into the kitchen till she leaves.

D: She?

(VALERIE enters through door at back of room.)

VALERIE: Shit. Ginger. *(She lies on floor and looks under the couch D is sitting on, calling for the cat.)* Ginge! Ginge! *(To D)* Ginger in here?

D: *(Blowing her nose)* The orange one? With the ear? *(She indicates bent ear.)*

VALERIE: Yes.

D: He's on the landing.

(VALERIE *runs off-stage, which leads to the downstairs of the house.*)

VALERIE: *(Shooing)* Whish. Whish. Whish. *(She exits. Her voice is heard.)* Downstairs. Whish. Whish. Whish.

D: She's nuts.

(A door slams downstairs.)

(VALERIE reenters.)

VALERIE: I've got Ginger locked in mother's bedroom, Molly in the kitchen. I don't know where Horace is. The one who sat on you. *(She runs to close door.)* If I leave the door open, he'll do it again. He likes strangers. *(She refers to D's allergy.)* Does that last long? Can I get you something for it?

D: It goes when the cats go.

VALERIE: Would you like lunch?

D: I don't know.

VALERIE: *(Matter of fact)* Well, are you hungry?

D: I ate a lot at the airport.

VALERIE: I need a sandwich. *(She starts to exit.)*

D: I can have a sandwich.

VALERIE: Do you eat ham?

D: I usually don't. I'm not kosher, but I usually don't eat ham.

VALERIE: Cheese?

D: Any'll be fine.

VALERIE: I'll bring it in here.

D: Can I help?

VALERIE: Then we'll have to deal with Horace.

(VALERIE exits, closing door behind her.)

(A spot light on D)

D: I couldn't see. I couldn't breathe. All I heard was my heart in my ears. There ought to be a law. No one should go to a reunion without a paid impartial observer. Someone to tell you what the hell happened!

VALERIE'S VOICE: Open the door.

(Living room lights up)

(D opens door.)

(VALERIE enters with tray: two sandwiches, two glasses of cranberry juice, and a plate of cookies. Neither of the women eats during their reunion.)

VALERIE: I can't find that cat. Close the door.
(She puts tray on coffee table and points to one sandwich.)
That's the cheese. *(She sits on couch with D.)*
You can live here if you want.

D: Live here?

VALERIE: If you want. That's cranberry juice.

D: I live in New York. I have a husband.
We live in the city. We're having a child.

VALERIE: When?

D: In the spring. A long time.

VALERIE: Kids like spring birthdays. I gave the class parties outside in the spring.

D: You teach?

VALERIE: I started teaching kindergarten.
I prefer twelfth.

D: You teach high school.

VALERIE: History. I've just retired. Twenty-seven years.
I liked it.

(D looks over to the laundry bags on the floor.)

(VALERIE rises and walks to bags.)

VALERIE: These are mother's things. She died before the summer. I brought them up here. I should have gotten them over to Goodwill. I was away this summer. *(She goes to desk.)* I have lots of pictures of her. Somewhere.

D: Do I look like her?

VALERIE: *(Nods)* You have Mickie's eyes.

D: My father?

VALERIE: Oh, yes, the seed. *(As an apology)*
People call me too straight at times. Forgive me.
(She sits.) Please, you want to ask me things.

D: Who was Mickie?

VALERIE: A sophomore at B.C., Catholic and horny.
He looked like Heathcliff.

D: The cat?

VALERIE: Cat? Oh, the cartoon cat. *(She laughs.)* No.
He looked like Bronte's Heathcliff. I wanted literary
passion in my life. We were together one night.
His family convinced him that he wasn't with me that
night, and I didn't want a man that didn't want me.

D: I look like him?

VALERIE: From what I remember. It's 35 years.

D: You never saw him again?

VALERIE: It's easy not to see people again, especially if
you don't know them well.

D: Mickie was his real name?

VALERIE: Michael.

D: My husband's name is Michael.

VALERIE: There are a lot of Michaels.

D: Him being Michael feels very weird.

VALERIE: Yes.

D: Did you know my mother? I mean, you know what I
mean.

VALERIE: I never met her.

D: Did you know we lived in Newton?

VALERIE: No.

D: Did you teach in Newton?

VALERIE: In Boston. The Boylston School. It's down the street from the hotel.

D: Oh.

VALERIE: *(Gently)* No. I didn't teach you.

(A cat scratches at door.)

VALERIE: Horace. *(The scratching stops.* VALERIE *crosses to her cigarettes.)* Smoke? *(D reaches for a cigarette.* VALERIE, *with her back to D, remembers that D doesn't smoke.)* No. That's right, you don't.

(D puts her hand down.)

D: I stopped a while ago.

VALERIE: This bother you?

D: No.

*(*VALERIE *returns cigarette to pack. She sees D's uneaten sandwich.)*

VALERIE: You don't have to eat what you don't want.

D: I'm waiting for my head to clear.

VALERIE: You've always been allergic?

D: Always.

VALERIE: *(Without thinking)* I don't know what I'd do if I was. I couldn't live without a cat in the house.

(A beat of silence. D blows her nose for the last time. VALERIE *walks to window.)*

VALERIE: Rain might be coming back again.

D: Why did you ask about ham?

VALERIE: I gave you to a Jewish agency.

D: Because you're Jewish.

VALERIE: Because I wanted you to have a good home.

D: Are you Catholic?

VALERIE: No. But my mother was brought up in Europe in a Catholic area, but she was a Protestant who married a Jew, whose family never went to synagogue,

which didn't bother him because he was an atheist.
And I end up being baptized at the Second Presbyterian
Church where I learned the Highland Fling in Sunday
school. But I left the church the day they put the spikes
over the front door to impale the pigeons.
Which should have been the end of my religious
education. But a girl in high school told everybody that
my father was Jewish and I was anti-Semitic since I
didn't practice the religion, which sent me to the library
where I learned all about Judaism and stayed home on
the holidays to the confusion of everyone in my family,
including myself.

(A cat scratches.)

VALERIE: Excuse me.

*(She starts to exit, then crosses back to get her cigarettes and
exits, closing door behind her.)*

(A spot light on D)

(D speaks to audience. She imitates VALERIE'S *voice.)*

D: *(In anger)* Easy not to see people, especially if you
don't know them well....I should have said: If he was
the seed and he wasn't responsible, then who were
you? The seed carrier? I mean, shit. Easy not to see
people if you don't know them well. And what do I
know about you, lady? Nothing. No problem not seeing
you again. You're gone! *(She imitates* VALERIE'S *gesture.)*
You went "Whish. Whish. Whish."

(Living room lights up)

*(VALERIE enters on D's last "whish". But she refers to her
cat.)*

VALERIE: That's unusual behavior.

(D turns to VALERIE.*)*

D: Pardon?

VALERIE: My mother named him. He misses her.
He's under the stairs. I don't see how I can show you
the rest of the house.

D: It's my only allergy.

VALERIE: Mother had hay fever which she called...
(VALERIE *uses a German accent.*) spring fever.
She was highly intelligent, but after living here fifty
years still invented her own English. She called Tom
Selleck Magnus P-One.

D: Was she from Germany?

VALERIE: Mother? Yes.

D: Were you born there too?

VALERIE: *(Shakes head)* She was pregnant when she came
over. I was born here in Newton. In this house.
She lived in the downstairs apartment. It's completely
private. It has its own entrance.

D: I live in New York.

(There is a beat of silence.)

D: Did she have only you?

VALERIE: I'm the only one.

D: And your father?

VALERIE: He died a long while back. All his relatives are
dead. My mother still has a sister living in East Berlin.
I met her for the first time this summer.

D: Is she very old?

VALERIE: *(Nods)* I'm the last. There's no one of that
family except me.

(The room darkens as the rain starts.)

(VALERIE turns on lamp.)

VALERIE: Do you have a profession?

D: I think of it more as a job...and I've taken so much
time off I wonder if I even have....I'm of that family.

VALERIE: You are. Of course.

D: At the hotel. You were there before me.

VALERIE: About ten minutes.

D: You said I looked like him.

VALERIE: I knew who you were. I can't explain.
Do you want me to try?

(D asks the question which has always been in the back of her mind.)

D: I want to know what happened in the hospital.

VALERIE: Hospital?

D: Camden Hospital.

VALERIE: Oh.... *(She speaks simply, without guilt.)*
I never saw you. I had anesthesia and never saw you.

D: How could you not see me?

VALERIE: I didn't want to.

D: They didn't let you?

VALERIE: I knew I'd never see you again, so I chose not
to.

(D gets a muscle cramp in leg. She hides the pain by sitting and trying to act casual.)

VALERIE: Your husband's name is Michael.

D: He's a writer. Non-fiction.

VALERIE: *(Offering cookies)* Mother baked. These are
supermarket.

D: No. Thank you.

VALERIE: I'm not a good cook.

D: Michael is.

VALERIE: I should have bought wine.

D: It looks like wine. *(The pain is getting stronger and D
cannot hide it anymore.)*

VALERIE: Is something wrong?

D: It's a cramp. It's no big deal.

VALERIE: Mother had a heating pad. *(She moves to exit for heating pad.)*

D: No. Thank you, no.

VALERIE: I'll give it to you.

D: I'm a hundred percent.

VALERIE: Let me get it for you.

D: I don't want it.

VALERIE: Please, let me.

D: I don't need it.

VALERIE: *(With force)* Please, let me give it to you.

D: Thank you.

(VALERIE puts uneaten food and drink on tray.)

VALERIE: Neither one of us wants these.

(VALERIE exits.)

(D stays seated, deep in thought.)

(Lights change to present, a winter afternoon.)

(MICHAEL enters, with energy and carrying three books.)

MICHAEL: D. The movers need to get in here. They need to know what you're selling.

(D jumps up.)

D: Not yet.

MICHAEL: She's gone. She's in Australia. Let's move this place!

(D pleads with MICHAEL.)

D: I haven't found anything yet. *(She runs to look through bookcase.)*

MICHAEL: There's nothing to find.

D: I need something to tell me why.

MICHAEL: You think everything has a reason. It doesn't. *(He shows D the three books.)* These are going home.

D: What are they?

MICHAEL: Three obscure Thackerays.

(D *takes books and looks through them.*)

D: From her bedroom?

MICHAEL: The bookcase on the middle landing.
What would be in them?

D: *(Looking through books)* Notes, letters,things in the
margins, flowers.

MICHAEL: They might be her mother's.

D: She was German.

MICHAEL: Leah listens to Strauss. She's Polish.

D: What does that mean?

MICHAEL: That a woman born in Germany can read
Thackeray.

D: She never said her mother liked Thackeray.

MICHAEL: Why should she tell you?

D: *(With emotion)* You don't understand.

MICHAEL: Her plans had to have been made before she
met you. You can't emigrate to Australia like that.
You have to have tickets, visas, permits....

D: Why do you always take her side?

MICHAEL: Don't put me in the middle of this.

D: You excuse her.

MICHAEL: I see a woman who wanted to meet you,
who saw a grown woman, who was having a baby of
her own, who had a life. She felt she could leave.

D: And why not tell me?

MICHAEL: She wrote you.

(D *gets letter.*)

D: This. This is a business letter.

MICHAEL: Accept it.

(D reads from letter.)

D: "I couldn't tell you that I was leaving for Australia.
I hope you will accept my house as a gift for the
baby...." Who she's going to see a lot of in Australia.

MICHAEL: She can write her grandchild.

D: *(Reads)* "Enclosed is my lawyer's number...."
Et cetera. Business. Et cetera. Business. And the
personal touch. "Forgive the shortness. I don't know
any other way."

MICHAEL: Not everyone is brave, D. *(A silent beat.
They are both on the verge of a fight.* MICHAEL *breaks the
silence.)* Why don't you call Leah. She wants to know
when we're coming back.

D: I can't call her from here.

MICHAEL: I'm going for something to eat. When I come
back, I want to know what you're going to keep and
what you're going to sell. We have a four-hour drive.
I don't want to get back late.

D: You don't understand.

MICHAEL: *(Releasing emotion)* That's right. I'll never
understand. So from now on wear shades when you're
around me.

D: Wear what?

MICHAEL: Shades, dark glasses, sun glasses. Shades on
all the motherless!

D: What are you...?

MICHAEL: Because it takes one look. One look from the
motherless and I'm paralyzed with instant guilt.
I've no more time for guilt. It keeps me doing for you.
And maybe I get 'off' doing for you. But I have no more
time for it. No more time for being afraid of you, afraid
of saying something that'll mess up your head more.
Because I don't have enough time to figure out what

kind of father I'm going to be. And to figure that out,
I need someone I can look in the eye.

D: I don't want to do that to you. I wanted something
here to change me.

MICHAEL: It doesn't work that way.

D: I'd be like you. Of all the people I'd like to change
into, it's you.

MICHAEL: *(Gently)* What do I have? I have a family.
I can talk about them. I can tell people my father's a
doctor. They have a big house in Riverdale and my
mother says "We live on Grosvenor Place, dear.
We don't pronounce the 's'." And I went to Dartmouth
like my brothers and my father. I know who I am.
And yet.... *(He takes a beat before he reveals himself to her.)*
And yet, I tell strangers I grew up across the train yards
on 207th. *(He imitates himself.)* "I didn't go to no private
school, man. I went to school at St. Jude's"....
And my father, who I say is dead, had a flats-fixed-here
yard with a sign "Mechanica En General." Everything I
saw on the express bus into Manhattan.

D: I didn't know. I didn't ask.

MICHAEL: I don't tell you much of what I need.

D: *(Goes to* MICHAEL*)* No. I give you such a small piece
back.

MICHAEL: Sometimes. *(A quiet beat, in which he puts his
hand on her belly.)*

D: She's not going to give a damn if her mother's
adopted.

MICHAEL: I hope not.

D: Name her.

MICHAEL: *(After a beat)* Consuelo.

D: Consuelo.

MICHAEL: Name him.

D: Tadeusz. ("Tah-day-oosh")

MICHAEL: Say it again.

D: Tadeusz. Leah's father.

MICHAEL: Tadeusz. If I can spell it. *(He leaps up in happiness and calls for the movers.)* Yo! Let's move this and get out of here. Yo. We can get started in here.

D: *(To MICHAEL, with love)* Yo.

(MOM and POP enter, carrying a chair. He is Boston Irish. She is Jamaican.)

POP: Were there cats in the house, Mr Cruz?

MICHAEL: What?

MOM: *(Showing chair)* You didn't tell us about the scratches.

MICHAEL: Yes. She had cats.

POP: When Mom and Pop make a deal, we make a deal. But next time you sell, don't sell without telling the buyers there were cats in the house.

(D stands in center of room and makes an announcement.)

D: I'm going to take the goddamn importance out of this goddamn place. I'm going to tell a joke!
Would you mind if I told a joke?

POP: It's your money.

MOM: I like jokes.

(They get in position to hear joke.)

D: This is a WASP joke. It's not what I wanted to tell. I wanted just a plain mother joke...for crazy reasons. But there aren't any. There are Italian mother jokes, Jewish mother jokes, mother-in-law jokes. Do you know there are no plain mother jokes in America?

MOM: Is this the joke?

MICHAEL: D.

D: Sorry. All right. *(She gets in 'joke position'.)* A man.
He's a WASP. He's married. A nice wife. Nice children.
A nice man who always sees his mother every Sunday.
He drives to Connecticut and they have lunch.
His mother and him. But one Sunday, his high school
lacrosse team is giving him an alumni award and he's
got to tell his mother he can't come. He's never missed
a lunch. And it's his birthday. So he calls his mother
and says, "Mother, I can't come for lunch this Sunday."
And she says, "Okay."

(MOM, POP, and MICHAEL stare at D, waiting for the punch line.)

D: That's the joke. She's says, "Okay." She doesn't say
what a Jewish mother would say. *(She laughs.)*
She's a WASP. She says "Okay." Okay.

POP: Mother's houses make you crazy.

MICHAEL: Mother's houses make you hungry.
I need food.

(D goes to MICHAEL, laughing.)

D: Nobody. Nobody gets this joke. "Okay."

MICHAEL: *(To D)* I need a bowl of chili.

*(POP and MOM join in the food 'thoughts' while they start to
move the furniture. MICHAEL moves coffee table to the side
and then he and POP lift couch.)*

POP: A meatball hero.

MOM: Codfish and bananas.

MICHAEL: Empanadas.

POP: Hash browns made in lard.

*(D sees MOM remove VALERIE's shawl from the back of her
chair. She has an unplanned, emotional reaction.)*

D: *(With force)* Stop. Don't touch that. Put that down.
*(MOM puts shawl back. D sees the coffee table has been
moved. She runs to it.)* I don't want anything removed
from this room. *(She returns coffee table to position.)*

This goes back where it was. (MICHAEL *and* POP *lower couch into position.*) I'm sorry. I don't mean to be rude.

(POP, *sensing her emotion, speaks gently.*)

POP: It's all right. We can wait.

MOM: Come on, Pop. We can do the downstairs.

(MOM *and* POP *exit.*)

D: *(To* MICHAEL, *with emotion)* I won't have this room empty. I won't let her go. She will stay in this room until I excuse her.

MICHAEL: Okay. Okay. *(He exits.)*

(*Lights change slowly to the October afternoon of* D's *visit with* VALERIE.)

(D *lets the depth of her emotion out. She speaks to* VALERIE *in her mind.*)

D: I'm not a piece of furniture! You can't throw me away! I was in Camden Hospital. I was in you. I don't forgive you.

(*We are back in the past.* VALERIE *enters with heating pad.* D's *emotion continues through her speech to* VALERIE.)

D: You can tell me what you want to tell me, and I can tell you what I want to tell you, or we don't have to tell each other anything, which may be unusual behavior. But I leave today. You seem to think I've come to live in your house or something. Well, I didn't come because I need something from you. I need nothing from you.

(VALERIE *reacts instinctively to* D's *anger.*)

VALERIE: Then don't stay!

(D *gets her coat.*)

D: I'm going.

VALERIE: I didn't mean that. I'd like you to stay. Please. (D *stops.*) You looked so like me.

D: I looked like you?

VALERIE: I didn't expect it and I should have. I never....
I simply didn't imagine you'd say you needed nothing.

D: I'm sorry. I didn't....

VALERIE: You mustn't apologize. I simply never
expected it. *(She stands by* D.) You see, when I let myself
dream of you, you were always standing in front of me,
looking up at me, and you'd say you needed something
from me. And I'd ask you what you needed and you'd
say, "You're the mother. You should know." I didn't
know. I never had an answer except feeling the pain of
having nothing to give you. And now, walking in,
I never imagined you'd look so like me. And that you
would say what I would have said if I'd been here,
waiting for a woman with too many cats to offer me a
heating pad, which is the last thing I'd come for.

*(*VALERIE *puts pad away.)*

D: *(With understanding)* Thank you for getting it for me.

VALERIE: I don't know if this will mean anything to
you. Last summer, I went to East Berlin to see our aunt.
I went to find out who Mother had been. We were very
close but I didn't know who she was besides my
mother. And I found out she was very much like me.
I'd always known that I had parts of her. But she never
let me know how much she was like me.

(There is a silent beat between the two women, VALERIE's
last line also having referred to D. VALERIE *reaches for D's
coat.* D *gives it to her.* VALERIE *puts coat down and turns to*
D.)

VALERIE: Do you travel?

D: I've been to Hawaii.

VALERIE: I taught so I could have the summers.

*(*VALERIE *gets stacks of envelopes containing post cards of
the places she's been to. She removes cards and puts stacks in
order on the floor.)*

(D stands in spot light.)

D: We sat on the floor together. She showed me post
cards of all the places she'd been. It took up most of the
afternoon. A man went on those trips with her. She said
"my friend". I kept thinking, "Was she sexy?" I mean,
with three cats and living with her mother.
And I decided, she was.

(Living room lights up)

(D kneels by VALERIE.*)*

VALERIE: *(Handing D post cards)* The Moselle Valley.
Wherever the river turns, you look back and see grapes,
like sunbathers leaning against a pole, facing the sun.
(She hands D another card.) The Seychelles. You go there
to find the moon. *(Another card)* Australia. This is Perth.
It's spring there now. Our October is their spring.
It's not a big city. It still has a pioneering spirit.
(A pause) All the rest are Australia. I don't know why I
always thought I was meant to be Australian. Always
dreamt it was my last frontier.... *(There is a beat in which
VALERIE decides she can't tell D she is leaving.)* Don't let
me bore you. *(She starts to put the cards back in envelope.)*

D: Oh no. *(Smiling)* Do you like Mel Gibson?

VALERIE: *(As to a girl friend)* Yes. He's nice.

D: Very nice.

(As VALERIE *puts cards back in envelope, D stands and goes
to window. It has gotten darker outside.)*

D: What time is it?

*(*VALERIE *has her back toward D and misinterprets D's
remark as her wanting to leave. She hides her disappointment
with a businesslike tone.)*

VALERIE: I'll drive you to the airport.

D: *(Surprised but polite)* I can take a cab.

VALERIE: 976-4000.

D: But if you want to drive, of course....

VALERIE: We're not going to stand here like women arguing over the check at Brigham's.

(Spot on D as she sits to dial.)

D: I meant it was getting dark. I didn't mean I wanted to go. Did she think I wanted to leave?

(Full lights on living room)

VALERIE: 976-4000.

(D dials.)

D: *(On phone)* I'm at 10 Cobble Street and I'm going to the airport....D Cruz....Five minutes!...Five minutes is fine. Thank you. *(She hangs up.)*

VALERIE: *(At window)* We can see the cab from here. The downstairs buzzer is broken. *(She crosses to laundry bags and opens one, going through the contents without removing them.)* She had a brocade bag. Small. Tapestry. *(She looks deeper in bag.)* Some kind of needlework. Perhaps a hundred years old. I'm not sure. I don't use things like that.

D: You don't have to....

VALERIE: We're not going to argue. *(She looks deeper in bag, finds a blouse of her mother's, takes it out and holds it.)* It was Proust, of course, who said.... *(Tears fill VALERIE's eyes. She lets the tears fall simply. She speaks when she is finished crying.)* I miss her. *(She laughs.)* I gave her as Irish a wake as a German can. My favorite one of hers is.... The day before my friend and I went to the Seychelles, we took mother to Revere Beach to see the fireworks. And every house we passed had a flag raised. And she said, "My goodness. There are flags up the kilt." And I said, "That must be pretty hard on the Scots, Mother." And she dismissed me as only Mother could and said, "You know, Valerie, to the tilt." She gave me five other variations, but never made it "Up to the hilt."

D: *(Laughs)* Flags up the kilt.

(The two women laugh together.)

(The cat scratches.)

VALERIE: Oh, Horace.

(VALERIE opens other bags, searching more energetically, but without removing the contents.)

D: Who was Tannenbaum?

VALERIE: *(While looking for purse)* I don't know which of us thought of that. It could have been her. For when I asked my aunt for all she knew about mother, the word she used most was "phantasie". "Sie hatte phantasie."

D: Fantasy?

VALERIE: Imagination. I found out that in school she never cared how her hair was combed. The back buttons of her skirt were always open. All she ever wanted was her friends to read Byron with her. Why didn't she let me know that wildness in her? Maybe it was me. Maybe I only smelled the cookies, saw the clean house, wore the ironed clothes. Then, of course, she got older and I took care of her. And then again, this is a house built for privacy. I can't remember who thought of Tannenbaum. We left here when I started to show. I can't even remember the street we stayed at.

D: 115 Pond Street.

VALERIE: *(Looking through bag)* Mother and I were on the top floor. Father'd come on weekends. I don't know which of us chose Tannenbaum.

(A horn honks.)

(VALERIE searches with more energy. D goes to window.)

D: I don't see the cab.

VALERIE: That was only a car. Sit. Sit. Please. *(She searches for gift.)* Tell me about your baby.

D: Michael and I think it's a girl.

(A car honks.)

VALERIE: That the cab?

(D goes to window.)

D: It is.

VALERIE: I wanted to give you that bag.

D: Thank you.

(The cab honks impatiently.)

(VALERIE shouts out window.)

VALERIE: We can hear you. *(She goes to D.)* I was born in this house and never left it. I didn't want to leave her. I'm 53. If I don't.... *(She cannot tell D she is leaving for Australia.)* I'll go down first and take care of the cats. I don't want you sneezing on the plane.

(VALERIE exits.)

D: I took the cab. She went to Australia. There is no answer here.

(Lights change to present.)

(D pulls chair to wall and removes pictures.)

D: *(Calling)* Mrs Eliat. Mr Eliat. I'm finished with the second floor.

(D wants nothing of VALERIE's. She removes VALERIE from her life by stripping the room of her belongings, building a pile of her things in the middle of room. When MOM and POP enter, they build on to that pile. They put the decorative items in cartons, move the furniture to the center, and place the cartons on top of it. The MOVERS, D, and MICHAEL work quickly and professionally.)

(MOM enters with cartons.)

MOM: You are ready for us now?

D: Please.

MOM: Have you made up your mind what you're taking with you?

D: I'm not taking anything.

(POP *speaks on entering.*)

POP: Can we get in here now?

MOM: She's not taking anything. It's all ours.

POP: *(To* D) Mr Cruz said there'd be a few items you were not selling.

D: I don't want anything. *(The* MOVERS *pack the cartons.)* What you think you won't sell, we'll bag for Goodwill. They're coming later to pick up those bags.
(She indicates laundry bags.)

(POP *speaks to* MICHAEL *as he enters room.*)

POP: She's not taking a thing.

MICHAEL: You're not?

D: I don't want anything.

MICHAEL: *(To Pop)* Well, then I guess it's all yours.

(MOM *finds envelope in bookcase and hands it to* MICHAEL, *who looks inside and gives it to* D.)

MICHAEL: Here.

(D *looks in envelope. It contains photographs.*)

D: They're pictures. She said she had pictures.

(As the MOVERS *and* MICHAEL *do their work around her,* D *excitedly goes through pictures.)*

D: Michael. This is the grapes place. The Valley.

(She follows MICHAEL, *showing him the pictures while he is helping the movers.)*

D: This must be the man who went with her.

MICHAEL: *(Looking at picture quickly)* Yeah.

D: Michael! This is her. They must be on vacation.

(He takes a quick look as he moves the coffee table to pile.)

MICHAEL: Good legs.

(D finds another picture.)

D: Michael.

MICHAEL: *(Meaning "I'm working")* D.

(D moves back to get out of MOM's *way and looks at pictures.* MICHAEL *and* POP *move couch to exact place she is standing.)*

MICHAEL: *(To* POP*)* How's your back?

POP: It's part of the job.

*(*MICHAEL *needs D to move so they can put down couch.)*

MICHAEL: D.

(D moves to another corner with her pictures.)

*(*POP *takes carton from* MOM *and places it on pile. The room is cleared of all decoration, including the curtains. With the furniture piled on top of each other, the room looks bare and unlived in.)*

POP: There are some papers you have to sign downstairs, Mr Cruz.

MICHAEL: I'll be down in a minute.

*(*MOM *and* POP *exit.)*

*(*MICHAEL *stands by D, who is holding pictures.)*

D: Is that my grandmother? *(She looks at back and finds name.)* Irmgard. It is. *(She looks at picture.)* I thought she'd be very fat. She's...God. Isn't she beautiful. She's really very beautiful.

MICHAEL: You have the same mouth.

D: *(Rejecting possibility)* No. *(She gets out another picture.)* This must be her as a baby. *(She looks at back of picture.)* It's Mr Baum. Kurt Baum bare-assed on a rug.... This little baby is our baby's great-grandfather. *(She goes back to her grandmother's picture.)* Her mouth is like my mouth?

MICHAEL: Same way it goes up.

(D looks at picture, allowing herself to accept that the beautiful grandmother's mouth is hers.)

D: It is my mouth. I have my grandmother's mouth.

MICHAEL: I better get downstairs. Why don't you call Leah? She wants to know when we're getting back.

(He exits.)

(D goes to phone, which is on floor. She begins to dial, then puts phone back on floor.)

D: I still have a fantasy. A "phantasie". Leah.

(Lights change to "fantasy".)

(LEAH's voice is heard.)

LEAH'S VOICE: Dorothy?

(D, shocked at hearing her mother's voice in VALERIE's house, quickly hides the pictures.)

D: Mother!

LEAH'S VOICE: Dorothy?

(D grabs her coat and runs downstairs to LEAH.)

(The lights for the scene have a warm, accessible tone. Even though the scene is ultimately a fantasy, it is performed with complete realism, making us forget it is a fantasy.)

(LEAH's and D's voices are heard. Their speeches overlap.)

D:	LEAH:
Mother! You've scared the life out of me. What are you doing here? Do you realize you have just scared the life out of me?	The door downstairs was open. I locked it. You shouldn't leave it open. The buzzer doesn't work. I was scared to death.

D: How did you get here?

LEAH: *(On entering)* A shuttle. A taxi.

(LEAH, wearing a bright red coat, walks into room with an energy we have not seen.)

D: I was just about to leave.

(LEAH walks directly to window.)

LEAH: I walked by this house when I went to see Carla. She lived on Linwood.

D: That's Linwood.

(LEAH *turns into room and looks at it for the first time. She is shocked that the room is bare*)

LEAH: You sold the furniture?

D: Yes. What are you doing here?

LEAH: I decided this morning.

D: I could have been gone.

LEAH: We didn't miss each other.

D: We didn't.

LEAH: Whose room is this?

(D *feels guilty, uncomfortable, finds it difficult to be with* LEAH *in her real mother's home.*)

D: Hers. Her mother had the downstairs.

(LEAH *goes to the laundry bags.*)

LEAH: I wanted to help you.

D: That's her mother's. She never got it to Goodwill.

LEAH: But you have photographs of her. Pictures of the family I can see.

D: No. She didn't leave any.

LEAH: She didn't leave you something personal?

D: She wanted to give me some kind of antique bag. Tapestry. It was her mother's. I didn't want it.

LEAH: Nothing for me to know?

D: I don't have anything to drink here. We can go to the doughnut shop on Walnut Street.

LEAH: You don't have to stay. I'll let myself out.

D: You look so different.

(D *crosses to* LEAH. LEAH *puts her hand on* D's *face.*)

LEAH: No. You stay. When you didn't ask me to come,
I asked myself. So. This is her house. *(She cries and is
angry with herself.)* What I said I wouldn't do.

D: *(Gently)* I didn't think you wanted to come.

LEAH: What I said I wouldn't do! *(She takes glasses off to
wipe eyes.)* So. When I take my glasses off, I see nothing.
It would be easier to be here if I didn't see, but I came to
see. *(She puts glasses on.)* So. This crazy mother.
I'm making you uncomfortable.

D: No. Yes.

LEAH: I'm Polish. I cry. Your father became New
England and he didn't like emotion either. And when
you were small and wanted to be picked up, and I
wanted so badly to hold you, and I thought you cried
for her, and I calmed you, and then I cried. All of which
I don't want to do today. So. This is hers. Did she have
books?

D: Yes.

(LEAH walks around room.)

LEAH: I sent away for the *World Book Encyclopedia* so
that the agency would see they were getting an
educational home and it came the day after our last
interview. And when it came and I read in it, I said, this
is not educational. This is cold like New England.
Written without life. But *Parents* magazine said get it.
I read *Parents* magazine before every interview.
The house smelled of furniture polish. My dress was
starched. My hair pulled back with many pins that kept
falling out I would try to pick them up when the social
worker wasn't looking. And there was an article called
"Why Fill Your Baby's Teeth". Foolish! But I told the
woman how important it was to fill a baby's first tooth.
All reading those articles did was to make me more
scared of you. So.... Next thing I am at LaGuardia.
Next thing I am here. I've never done something like

this before. Even marrying Howard I thought about before I did it. *(To* D*)* And you told me nothing about her.

D: I don't know anything.

LEAH: I didn't come to make you nervous. I came to see. And there is nothing.

D: Mother, it's over. I sold everything.

LEAH: Everything is out of all the rooms?

*(*LEAH *goes through door into back rooms.)*

D: Yes. *(She follows* LEAH.*)* Let's go home.

*(*LEAH *re-enters.)*

LEAH: What were her books?

D: Mother.

LEAH: Were there letters in the books? Flowers?

D: I sold them.

LEAH: What did you sell?

D: Pots, lamps, umbrellas, towels.

LEAH: What did you keep?

D: Nothing.

LEAH: Let me know. Tell me.

D: I don't have anything to tell!

*(*D *crosses to window, looks out, hiding her face from* LEAH.*)*

LEAH: Since you saw her, your eyes turn from me. You look into store windows. You make believe you don't see me on Broadway.

D: *(Not looking at* LEAH*)* She went to a Scottish church. She gave me a cheese sandwich. She didn't need me. She left.

LEAH: I want to know. Tell me. Tell me what you can't tell me.

*(*D *turns to* LEAH.*)*

D: I have a father somewhere. She spent one night with him. I have his eyes.... I had a grandmother. She was from Germany. She was wild when she was young and very beautiful. I have her mouth.

(LEAH *confronts* D *with what both of them have always been afraid to talk about. It is the most difficult part of* D's *experience to tell* LEAH. *She is filled with emotion.*)

LEAH: Tell me about your mother.

D: She liked Mel Gibson. We sat on the floor together. In here. She told me I was like her. She didn't look like a mother. She looked too young. (D *allows her love for* VALERIE *to be revealed.*) She looked more like a...friend. I have pictures. Do you want to see them?

LEAH: No.

(D *takes tissue out of pocket and gently dries* LEAH's *forehead.*)

D: Your forehead's all wet.

LEAH: I sweat. Ladies don't sweat.... Your tissues don't smell of cigarettes anymore. You were very brave to stop.... (*She puts her hands on* D's *arms.*) I'm sorry. I should have....

D: You don't have....

LEAH: Let me. I should have pulled you to me when I saw you looking away from me on Broadway. (*She crosses away.*) She makes me act like a child. Like I am her child too. Because SHE is the mother.

(D *goes to* LEAH.)

D: You are.

LEAH: (*Points to her head*) Up here I know I am. (LEAH *gestures to room.*) And I've talked it out with her so many times. But she always stopped our talk when she told me how it felt with you inside her. And I would remember you came to me through a telephone call.

D: But I was put down in the warm place where the pin was.

LEAH: Yes. It's a lovely story.

D: It's a story?

LEAH: *(Quickly)* No. It's real. I found the pin the day they called me. *(She goes to laundry bags.)* These are her mother's things?

D: Yes.

LEAH: Go to the doughnut shop.

(LEAH opens the bags, tossing the contents on the floor.)

D: Mother, what are you doing? You're throwing everything on the floor! Goodwill is going to be here any minute. Mother! Why don't you just turn them upside down?!

LEAH: Much better. *(She dumps contents of last bag on floor.)*

D: You're going to put every one of those things back in.

LEAH: Fine. *(LEAH finds grandmother's tapestry bag.)* This is it! This is it! *(She hands bag to D.)* Here.

D: Thank you.

LEAH: All our lives we would have thought about that bag. *(She sits on arm of couch.)* So. I have just done something Margaret Sullavan would have done.

(D finds an empty space and joins her. They are surrounded by cartons and furniture.)

D: Who's Margaret Sullavan?

LEAH: She was a movie star. She was very famous.

D: Before I was born?

LEAH: On the year you were born. That's when I saw the movie. It was after one of the Agency interviews, and I know the social worker saw I was sweating. What questions they ask you. If I had come to terms with my sterility? Those were her words. Of course,

you say I have. I don't think you ever come to terms
with it. You live with it. A small lie for a baby. So.
I go to see Margaret Sullavan and she's got cancer.
In the movie, not life. And in one scene she sees the
woman who works for her husband...and who is falling
hopelessly in love with her husband. So the woman is
packing because if she stays any longer she will be
more hopelessly in love with the husband.
And Margaret Sullavan says "Stay!" By doing that she
takes care of her husband after she dies. I knew I could
never be that good.

D: I used to think the bad ones got adopted and the
good ones got kept.

LEAH: And I thought the good ones had babies.

D: Can one want a baby and think one doesn't?

(LEAH *gets up and puts clothes back in bags.*)

LEAH: The head is not always the most intelligent part.

(D *crosses to* LEAH.)

D: *(Refers to baby)* She's the one who brought me here.
Or he. Tadeusz.

(LEAH *is deeply moved. After a beat, she hugs* D. *They stay
together for a beat.*) So. (*She refers to furniture and bags.*)
We leave this?

D: The neighbor has the key.

(*The women pack the laundry bags.*)

D: I didn't want you to know she didn't need me.

LEAH: No more of her. We'll finish and go someplace
nicer than a doughnut shop.

D: I feel a baby inside me and it doesn't automatically
make me a mother.

LEAH: No more.

D: Mother! This is the first time in our lives that we are
talking.

LEAH: We have done too much of this talking silently to each other. I say no more. I am taking you to get a permanent.

(During LEAH's *speech, the women finish packing the bags and put on their coats)*

D: A permanent?

LEAH: I had one. It made me look like a lion.
I'm not good with hair. You went to Suzy's mother to have your hair done. But I looked beautiful with my permanent when I came out of the beauty parlor.
For the first time a lady. And I washed it and I was no more a lady, but a lion. I didn't know what to do.
How my hair looked when I woke up in the morning was how it looked all day. Howard said, "Wash it out. Wash what they put in your hair out." I'd say, "This is washing!" And the only thing to do was to go to a beauty parlor once a week and have them sit on it.
But that was expensive and I don't like beauty parlors...everywhere mirrors. So I put a kerchief on my head if I had to go see Howard at the store. But what do you think? I liked it! I liked the wildness. I had hair!
Everything would be fine if I didn't have to see it. But I could put my hand out to here and feel hair. I felt taller.
Younger, like her. I felt very sexy, too. And I didn't think about you all the time. I am to blame I didn't get another. But now when I listen to Strauss I feel that way. So. This is me. Now, I can go from here.

D: Will you show me what to do when the baby comes?

LEAH: I will show you.

D: So.

LEAH: So.

*(*LEAH *exits.)*

(Lights change to the present.)

D: No. I have to come to you.

(D *goes to phone. She dials. We hear a ring.*)

(LEAH *enters. It is the* LEAH *from Act One. She sits and answers her phone, which is at the corner of the stage.*)

D: *(On phone)* It's me.

LEAH: Are you back in the city?

D: I'm in Newton. I've just finished packing. We're going to get something to eat.

LEAH: So.

D: So I wanted to let you know I'm on my way back.

LEAH: I'll see you then.

D: *(With love)* Yes. I'll come to you.

(D *hangs up phone.* LEAH *hangs up phone.*)

(D *picks up her photographs and the tapestry bag.*)

(*She crosses the stage into* LEAH's *area.*)

(LEAH *stands waiting for her.*)

D: Hello.

LEAH: Hello.

END OF PLAY